Contents

The Ten Commandments

Words to Use

Moses

Sinai

Egypt

mountain

two

Ten Commandments

slavery

1. God's people once lived in the land of

_____.

2. God's people once lived under the control

of others in _____.

3. After God rescued His people, He brought

them to a _____.

4. _____ was the name of the place

where God talked to Moses.

5. God gave the commandments to

_____ and to God's people.

6. God wrote the commandments on

_____ pieces of stone.

7. In all God wrote _____

_____.

According to God's Word

1. God gave us the Ten Commandments

because He (loves—fears) us.

2. The commandments tell us how to

(covet—live).

3. God sent (Moses—Jesus) to earn forgive-

ness for the times we break the command-

ments.

In Words of My Own

1. Describe God coming down to the moun-

tain to give Moses and the people the Ten

Commandments.

_____

_____

2. What is God like?

_____

_____

3. Why did God give us the Ten Command-

ments?

_____

_____

_____

My First Catechism
Activity Book

CONCORDIA PUBLISHING HOUSE · SAINT LOUIS

Copyright © 2005 Concordia Publishing House

3558 S. Jefferson Ave., St. Louis, MO 63118-3968

1-800-325-3040 · www.cph.org

Prepared and edited by Rodney L. Rathmann

This publication may be available in braille, in large print, or on cassette tape for the visually impaired. Please allow 8 to 12 weeks for delivery. Write to the Library for the Blind, 7550 Watson Rd., St. Louis, MO 63119-4409; call toll-free 1-888-215-2455; or visit the Web site: www.blindmission.org.

Manufactured in the United States of America

6 7 8 9 10   20 19 18 17 16

The First Commandment

Words to Use

angel

king

statue

worship

furnace

1. A wicked _____ once ordered the people to worship an idol he had made.

2. The idol was in the form of a _____.

3. Three men who believed in God refused to _____ any god but the true God.

4. The three who believed in God were thrown into a _____.

5. God sent His _____ to save the three men.

According to God's Word

1. Three (men—statues) trusted in the true God.

2. (God—the king) saved the three men.

3. "Come out of the furnace!" called the king. "There is no god like your God. He (trusts—saves) His people!"

In Words of My Own

1. What does it mean to worship?

_____

_____

2. What things do you sometimes allow to take God's place?

_____

_____

_____

_____

3. When has God saved you?

_____

_____

_____

_____

_____

The First Commandment

Words to Use

Isaac

ram

altar

Jesus

Abraham

1. _____ had a son named Isaac.

2. Both _____ and his father were willing to obey God.

3. God tested Abraham's faith by asking him to sacrifice his son on an _____.

4. God provided a _____ for the sacrifice.

5. _____ willingly sacrificed Himself to save us.

According to God's Word

1. Once God told a father and son to travel to a (river—mountaintop).

2. Here a (sacifice—bargain) was to be made.

3. God (tested—took) Abraham's faith.

4. (God—Jesus) is the father who sacrificed His Son to pay for the sins of the world.

In Words of My Own

1. What does it mean to sacrifice?

   _____

   _____

   _____

2. Explain the relationship between having faith and obeying.

   _____

   _____

   _____

   _____

   _____

3. What does Jesus' sacrifice mean to you?

   _____

   _____

   _____

   _____

   _____

   _____

The Second Commandment

Words to Use

slingshot

Goliath

David

giant

shepherd

1. A _____ once came out onto a battlefield where he spoke against God and His people.

2. When David came out onto the battlefield, _____ cursed him.

3. David was a _____ boy.

4. David killed the giant using a _____.

5. _____ trusted in God.

According to God's Word

1. The giant wanted someone to (trust—fight) him.

2. The giant (cursed—defeated) David.

3. David told the giant, "I come against you in the (sight—name) of the Lord Almighty.

4. When the (slingshot—stone) hit the giant in the forehead, he fell dead.

In Words of My Own

1. What does it mean to do something in the name of the Lord?

_____

_____

_____

2. In what way does David battling Goliath remind you of Jesus facing the devil in order to save us?

_____

_____

_____

_____

_____

_____

3. What does it mean to trust in the Lord?

_____

_____

_____

The Second Commandment

Words to Use

men

lions

angel

Daniel

king

1. _____ loved God.

2. Evil _____ tricked the king.

3. The lions never touched Daniel because of the _____ God had sent to protect him.

4. The king knew that God had saved Daniel from the _____.

5. The happy _____ proclaimed, "The God of Daniel is the living God."

According to God's Word

1. Daniel prayed to God (three—ten) times a day.

2. The king passed a (sign—law) saying that no one should pray to God.

3. Daniel never stopped (praying—explaining) to God.

4. The king said, "The God of Daniel is the (arresting—living) God.

In Words of My Own

1. How has God saved you?

   _____

   _____

   _____

2. If you were Daniel, what prayer would you offer after being taken out of the lions' den?

   _____

   _____

   _____

   _____

The Third Commandment

Words to Use

twelve

three

temple

Passover

Jerusalem

1. Jesus was _____ years old when he went with Mary and Joseph to Jerusalem.

2. The _____ celebration was held in Jerusalem.

3. When Mary and Joseph couldn't find Jesus, they went once again to _____.

4. They searched for Jesus for _____ days.

5. Finally they found Jesus with the teachers in the _____.

According to God's Word

1. Clearly, Jesus loved being in (danger—the temple).

2. Jesus spoke of being in His (Father's—Mother's) house.

3. Jesus was found listening to the (entertainers—teachers) and asking them questions.

In Words of My Own

1. What was Jesus' attitude about spending time at the temple? How do you know?

_____

_____

_____

_____

_____

2. In what way is Jesus' Father the same as your father?

_____

_____

_____

_____

3. What do you and others see and do when you are in God's house?

_____

_____

_____

_____

_____

The Third Commandment

Words to Use

worried

chosen

working

listening

important

1. Martha was busy _____ to make Jesus' visit pleasant and enjoyable.

2. Mary was _____ to Jesus' words.

3. Jesus said that Martha was _____ about many things.

4. Jesus told Martha that one thing is _____.

5. Mary had _____ to hear Jesus' words.

According to God's Word

1. Mary and Martha were (sisters—friends).

2. Martha wanted (Jesus—Mary) to come and help her.

3. Jesus said that (referring—listening) to God's Word is the one important thing.

In Words of My Own

1. Was Martha wrong to serve Jesus as she did? Why or why not?

_____

_____

_____

_____

2. Why is Mary's choice the right choice?

_____

_____

_____

_____

3. When do you listen to God's Word?

_____

_____

_____

_____

_____

_____

The Fourth Commandment

Words to Use

save

holy

disobey

obey

help

1. Jesus is _____.

2. He came to earth to _____ all people.

3. As the Son of God, He was able to _____ His parents in all things.

4. As Jesus grew, He became more and more of a _____ to His parents.

5. Because of Jesus, we are forgiven for the times we _____ our parents.

According to God's Word

1. The Fourth Commandment tells us to (honor—worship) our parents.

2. Jesus was once (an angel—a baby).

3. Jesus lived a perfect (life—lie) in our place.

4. Jesus obeyed His (Father—Mother) in heaven.

5. Jesus never (lied—spoke) to Mary and Joseph.

In Words of My Own

1. What does it mean to honor one's parents?

   _____

   _____

   _____

2. What did Jesus do for us in our place because we are unable to do it?

   _____

   _____

   _____

   _____

   _____

The Fourth Commandment

Words to Use

army
head
justice
handsome
forgiveness

1. Absalom was a _____ man.

2. Absalom told the people that if he were king, the people would get _____.

3. King David wanted to show love and _____ to Absalom.

4. Absalom led an _____ against his father David.

5. Absalom died after his _____ became caught in a tree.

According to God's Word

1. Absalom suggested to the people that he would make a good (king—soldier).

2. Absalom rode a (mule—camel) to escape from David's soldiers.

3. The (rear guard—commander) of David's army killed Absalom.

4. At the death of Absalom, David felt (relieved—sad).

In Words of My Own

1. How did Absalom sin against the Fourth Commandment?

_____

_____

_____

2. How did David show himself to be a parent who loves the Lord?

_____

_____

3. Why do God's people show love and forgiveness to others?

_____

_____

_____

_____

The Fifth Commandment

Words to Use

farmer

shepherd

offering

best

jealous

1. One of the sons of Adam and Eve, Cain, became a _____.

2. Abel, their other son, became a _____.

3. Both brought their _____ to the Lord.

4. Abel gave to God from among the _____ that he had.

5. Cain became _____ and killed his brother.

According to God's Word

1. God gave Adam and Eve sons after they left the (town—garden) of Eden.

2. (The sons—Eve) brought gifts to God.

3. God was (angry—pleased) with Abel's offering.

4. Jesus, the Savior of the world, came from (Seth's—Cain's) family.

5. To murder someone is to (call—kill) that person.

In Words of My Own

1. How does the story of Cain and Abel show that one sin often leads to another?

_____

_____

_____

2. How does the way Cain and Abel brought their gifts to God differ from how we give God our offerings?

_____

_____

_____

_____

_____

_____

3. Why did Jesus come into the world?

_____

_____

_____

_____

The Fifth Commandment

Words to Use

thieves
story
enemy
help
wounds

1. Jesus once told a _____.

2. Jesus told about a man who was attacked by _____.

3. The person who helped the wounded man was really his _____.

4. The man who came to help bandaged the injured man's _____.

5. Like the man who showed kindness, Jesus came to _____ and save us.

According to God's Word

1. In Jesus' story a man traveled from (Jerusalem—Bethlehem) to Jericho.

2. Some thieves robbed and (insulted—wounded) the man.

3. The thieves left the man half (awake—dead).

4. Samaritans and (Jesus—Jews) were enemies.

5. The Good Samaritan reminds us of (the wounded man—Jesus).

In Words of My Own

1. According to the Fifth Commandment, how does God want us to treat other people?

_____

_____

_____

2. Of whom does the wounded man remind us? Explain.

_____

_____

_____

_____

_____

3. In what ways is Jesus like the Good Samaritan?

_____

_____

_____

_____

_____

_____

The Sixth Commandment

Words to Use

forgive

sin

stone

adultery

ground

1. _____ is a sin that misuses God's gift of marriage.

2. The people asked Jesus whether they might _____ the woman.

3. To make a point, Jesus wrote on the _____.

4. Jesus said that the person without _____ should throw the first stone.

5. Jesus was willing to _____ the woman.

According to God's Word

1. (Teachers—Students) brought to Jesus a woman who had been unfaithful to her husband.

2. Jesus wrote on the ground using a (stick—finger).

3. The people began to leave until only Jesus and the (man—woman) remained.

4. Jesus (forgave—scolded) the woman.

5. "(Have—Leave) your life of sin," Jesus told the woman.

In Words of My Own

1. In Old Testament times, how were people who committed adultery to be punished?

_____

_____

2. How did Jesus treat the woman who had sinned?

_____

_____

_____

3. How does Jesus treat us when we sin?

_____

_____

_____

_____

The Sixth Commandment

Words to Use

almighty

marriage

wife

change

husband

1. Because Jesus is God, He has the power to _____ things.

2. Once Jesus attended a wedding where He showed His _____ power by changing water into wine.

3. God wants husbands and wives to be happy in their _____.

4. Jesus' love for those who believe in Him is like that of a _____ for his wife.

5. Jesus reminds us of someone willing to give his life for his _____.

According to God's Word

1. Once Jesus attended a wedding in (Jerusalem—Cana).

2. Jesus' (mother—servant) was also at the wedding.

3. At the wedding Jesus showed that He was (thirsty—God).

4. Jesus used His power to make (water—wine).

In Words of My Own

1. Jesus once provided refreshments for people at a wedding. For which of the things Jesus has provided you are you especially thankful today?

_____

_____

_____

_____

_____

2. At the wedding in Cana, how did Jesus show Himself to be God?

_____

_____

_____

3. God wants husbands and wives to love one another as Jesus loves all people. Describe this kind of love.

_____

_____

_____

_____

_____

_____

The Seventh Commandment

Words to Use

victory

stole

promised

forgive

hidden

1. God brought His people safely into the land He had _____ them.

2. God brought the people _____ over Jericho.

3. Achan disobeyed; he _____ things for himself.

4. Nothing can be _____ from God.

5. Jesus died to _____ all sins.

According to God's Word

1. God told the people not to (take — destroy) anything from the city of Jericho.

2. Achan (obeyed—disobeyed) God.

3. Achan (hid—sold) the things he had taken from Jericho.

4. Jesus (ignores—forgives) all sins, including the sin of stealing.

In Words of My Own

1. What is stealing?

_____

_____

_____

2. What kinds of things do people steal from one another?

_____

_____

_____

_____

3. How can we be sure that we can be forgiven for stealing?

_____

_____

_____

_____

_____

The Seventh Commandment

Words to Use

heart

taxes

possessions

cheated

short

1. Zacchaeus was very rich; he was also

   _____.

2. Zacchaeus worked collecting people's

   _____.

3. Jesus changed the _____ of

   Zacchaeus.

4. Zacchaeus promised to give half his

   _____ to the poor.

5. Zacchaeus said that if he had

   _____ anyone, he would repay

   four times the amount.

According to God's Word

1. Zacchaeus was a (poor—rich) collector of

   taxes.

2. Zacchaeus wanted to see (Jesus—a

   sycamore-fig tree).

3. Jesus (changed—scared) Zacchaeus.

In Words of My Own

1. How has Jesus changed you?

   _____

   _____

   _____

   _____

2. What did Jesus mean when He said, "I
   have come to seek and save the lost"?

   _____

   _____

   _____

   _____

The Eighth Commandment

Words to Use

evidence

false

trial

truth

1. Jesus' enemies brought Him to stand _____ before the leaders of the day.

2. The court needed _____ in order to put Jesus to death.

3. Though many witnesses came before the court, their statements about Jesus were all _____.

4. When the chief priest asked Jesus whether He was the Christ, the Son of God, Jesus spoke the _____.

According to God's Word

1. The false witnesses did not (fight—agree) with one another.

2. The chief priest asked Jesus (directly—secretly) if He was the Son of God.

3. When Jesus spoke, He always spoke (kindly—the truth).

4. Jesus' words made the chief priest (happy—angry).

In Words of My Own

1. Why is it strange that Jesus was placed on trial?

_____

_____

2. Why was Jesus willing to suffer persecution, arrest, and trial?

_____

_____

_____

_____

_____

3. Why is it important to you that Jesus answered the chief priest's question with "Yes"?

_____

_____

_____

The Eighth Commandment

Words to Use

well

enemy

friend

defend

1. Jonathan was David's _____.

2. King Saul treated David as an

   _____.

3. Jonathan spoke _____ of David.

4. Jonathan spoke to _____David

   before Saul.

According to God's Word

1. King Saul (loved—hated) David.

2. Jonathan gave David (gifts—trouble).

3. Jonathan spoke (well—evil) of David

   before King Saul.

4. Jonathan's love for David reminds us of

   the love (David—Jesus) has for us.

In Words of My Own

1. By what kinds of words do we break the
   Eighth Commandment?

   _____

   _____

   _____

2. What message does Jesus bring to His
   Father about us and our sins?

   _____

   _____

   _____

   _____

3. What gifts has your friend Jesus given to
   you?

   _____

   _____

   _____

   _____

The Ninth Commandment

Words to Use

vineyard

crime

sulked

planned

brooded

1. Ahab coveted the _____
   of Naboth.

2. Ahab _____ and _____
   when Naboth refused to sell the vineyard
   to him.

3. Jezebel _____ an evil scheme
   to get the vineyard for Ahab.

4. Jezebel told people to lie by saying that
   Naboth had committed a _____.

According to God's Word

1. Those who told lies about Naboth broke
   the (Eighth—Seventh) Commandment.

2. Naboth's death was a sin against the
   (Fifth—Sixth) Commandment.

3. Jesus died to earn (justice—forgiveness) for
   all sins, including the sins of Ahab and
   Jezebel.

In Words of My Own

1. Sometimes one sin leads a person to commit still others. Explain this truth using the
   example in the story of Naboth's vineyard.

   _____

   _____

   _____

2. What does it mean to covet?

   _____

   _____

   _____

   _____

3. How did Jesus earn forgiveness of all sins,
   including the sin of coveting?

   _____

   _____

   _____

The Ninth Commandment

Words to Use

nephew

rescue

reward

tenth

possessions

1. Lot was a _____ of Abraham.

2. Abraham rescued Lot and his neighbors and their _____.

3. The king wanted to give Abraham a _____.

4. Instead of receiving things, Abraham gave things to God; Abraham gave Melchizedek a _____ of all he had acquired in battle.

5. Long after the time of Abraham, God sent Jesus to _____ us and all people.

According to God's Word

1. Once enemies came to carry away the (people—leaders) of Sodom and their possessions.

2. After Abraham rescued the people, the king wanted to give Abraham a (city—reward).

3. Abraham (refused—accepted) the king's offer.

4. Abraham gave God gifts, presenting them to (Melchizedek—Sodom).

5. God sent Jesus to give us salvation—the greatest (gift—enemy) of all.

In Words of My Own

1. How do the actions of Abraham differ from those of Ahab and Jezebel?

   _____

   _____

   _____

   _____

2. When and where do you give God your offerings of thanks?

   _____

   _____

   _____

3. In what ways has Jesus rescued you?

   _____

   _____

   _____

The Tenth Commandment

Words to Use

terrible

repented

husband

coveted

prophet

1. David set into motion a plan to kill Bathsheba's _____ .

2. The _____ Nathan came to call David to account because of his sin.

3. David's sin was _____.

4. David _____ the wife of another man.

5. When David _____, God forgave him for Jesus' sake.

According to God's Word

1. David looked out from his (palace—temple) and saw Bathsheba.

2. David (coveted—hated) Bathsheba.

3. David broke the (Fifth—Sixth) commandment when he had Bathsheba's husband killed.

4. David broke the (Fifth—Sixth) commandment when he interfered with Bathsheba's marriage.

5. In response to Nathan's accusation, David (repented—rejoiced).

In Words of My Own

1. In what way did Jesus pay for all the terrible things all people have done?

   _____

   _____

   _____

2. What comfort does Jesus bring to all who repent of their sin?

   _____

   _____

   _____

The Tenth Commandment

Words to Use

submit

disrespect

serve

rest

1. Sarah treated Hagar poorly, and Hagar treated Sarah with _____.

2. As Hagar was running away, she sat down by a spring to _____.

3. At the well, the angel of the Lord came to Hagar and told her to go back and _____ to Sarah.

4. Just as Jesus loves and serves us, He leads us to love, _____, and submit to one another.

According to God's Word

1. Abraham's wife was named (Sarah—Hagar).

2. Hagar was running away when she came to a spring in the (forest—desert).

3. The angel of the Lord told Hagar to go back to Sarah. "(Abraham—God) will bless you," the angel said.

4. (Hagar—Sarah) did as the angel had said.

5. God sent Jesus to pay for the (wrongs—favors) we have done.

In Words of My Own

1. According to the explanation of the Tenth Commandment, how does God want people to treat one another?

_____

_____

_____

_____

2. After urging her to return and do her duty, what promise did the angel give to Hagar?

_____

_____

_____

3. Why do God's people love, serve, and submit to one another?

_____

_____

_____

_____

The Close of the Commandments

Words to Use

walked

wicked

outside

grief

inside

1. The behavior of the people filled God's heart with _____.

2. Noah loved God; the Bible says that Noah _____ with God.

3. God sent a flood; everything _____ the ark was saved.

4. God destroyed every living thing _____ the ark.

According to God's Word

1. God told Noah to (buy—build) an ark, a large boat.

2. God told Noah to assemble his (family—neighbors) and two of every kind of animal inside the ark.

3. God sent a flood to (destroy—save) every living thing outside the ark.

In Words of My Own

1. Noah and his family were also sinners. Why didn't God destroy them?

   _____

   _____

   _____

   _____

   _____

2. In what way does the ark remind you of the church?

   _____

   _____

   _____

   _____

   _____

   _____

The Close of the Commandments

Words to Use

worshiped
landed
blessed
safe
reminded

1. God kept Noah, his family, and all the animals with them _____ inside the ark.

2. As the floodwaters receded, the ark _____ on a mountaintop.

3. After Noah and his family left the ark, they _____ God.

4. The rainbow God placed into the sky _____ Noah, his family, and their descendants that God would never again destroy the world with a flood.

5. God _____ Noah and his descendants.

According to God's Word

1. God punishes sin. He once (destroyed—blessed) the world with a flood.

2. God placed a rainbow in the sky as a sign of His (grace—threats) and promises.

3. God gave Noah and his descendants a (new—perfect) life after the flood.

In Words of My Own

1. To whom does God promise "grace and every blessing"?

   _____

   _____

   _____

2. What new life do all people receive when they come to faith in Jesus?

   _____

   _____

   _____

   _____

3. In what way have you received a new life through water?

   _____

   _____

   _____

   _____

The Apostles' Creed

Words to Use

born
Trinity
conceived
worship

1. Jesus was _____ by the Holy Spirit.

2. Jesus was _____ to a young woman named Mary.

3. Wise Men followed a star so they might _____ the Savior.

4. The true God is the _____.

According to God's Word

1. Jesus was born of the (Virgin—widow) Mary.

2. We believe in the holy Trinity, (three—many) persons, yet only one God.

3. God gives (sudden—spiritual) wisdom to those who trust in Him.

4. God wants all people to be (saved—crucified) and to come to a knowledge of the truth.

In Words of My Own

1. How would you describe the true God?

_____

_____

_____

_____

2. Name the three persons in the Trinity.

_____

_____

3. Explain how your Savior is both God and man.

_____

_____

_____

_____

4. What is God's desire for all people?

_____

_____

_____

The First Article

Creation

Words to Use

rested

Eden

created

heaven

1. When God made all things from nothing, He _____ them.

2. After making all things in just six days, God _____.

3. God gave Adam and Eve a beautiful garden home called _____.

4. One day all who believe in Jesus will live in a beautiful home called _____.

According to God's Word

1. God made all things including the (sun—sin).

2. God made the first people, Adam and (Eden—Eve).

3. The home of the first people was a beautiful (house—garden).

4 There was no (sun—sin) in paradise.

5. Because we know Jesus as our (Savior—Creator), one day we will live with Him in a happy home.

In Words of My Own

1. How was life for Adam and Eve in the garden different from life in our world?

_____

_____

_____

_____

2. What will heaven be like?

_____

_____

3. What unique qualities and abilities has God the Father given you?

_____

_____

_____

4. Describe the new life God the Father has given you in Jesus.

_____

_____

_____

_____

The Second Article

Redemption

Words to Use

crucified

Second

only

right

judge

ascended

born

1. Jesus is the _____ Son of God.

2. The work and person of Jesus are described in the _____ Article.

3. Jesus came to earth when He was conceived by the Holy Spirit and _____ of the Virgin Mary.

4. Jesus paid for my sins with His life when He was _____.

5. Jesus left the earth when He _____ into heaven.

6. Now He sits at the _____ hand of God, the Father.

7. One day Jesus will come to earth again to _____ the living and the dead.

According to God's Word

1. Jesus was (conceived—begotten) of the Father from eternity.

2. Jesus is both true (God—devil) and true man, the son of Mary.

3. I believe that by nature I am a(n) (innocent—lost) person.

4. Jesus redeemed me with His (gold—blood).

In Words of My Own

1. From what three evils has Jesus rescued you?

   _____

   _____

2. What does Jesus empower you to do as you live under Him in His kingdom?

   _____

   _____

   _____

3. What does it mean to you that Jesus has risen from the dead and that He lives and reigns to all eternity?

   _____

   _____

   _____

   _____

   _____

And in Jesus Christ His only Son, our Lord.

Words to Use

Easter

die

holy

punishment

1. Jesus lived a _____ life in my place.

2. Jesus came to earth to _____ for my sins and the sins of all people.

3. Jesus took our _____ upon Himself.

4. Jesus rose from the dead on _____.

According to God's Word

1. Jesus came to earth to live a (sinless—sinful) life for us.

2 Jesus showed Himself to be true (God—man) when He died on the cross.

3. Jesus is (true God—true man—both true God and true man).

In Words of My Own

1. Why did Jesus have to obey God in our place?

_____

_____

_____

2. What punishment did Jesus take in our place?

_____

_____

_____

3. What does it mean for us that Jesus rose from the dead?

_____

_____

_____

_____

_____

Who was conceived by the Holy Spirit.

Words to Use

Son
servant
angel
mother
message

1. The _____ Gabriel came to Mary.

2. Gabriel brought Mary a _____.

3. Mary asked how she could be a

   _____ .

4. Mary was to give birth to the _____
   of God.

5. Mary called herself the Lord's _____.

According to God's Word

1. Gabriel told Mary she was highly
   (favored—worshiped).

2. Mary would be the mother of the Son of
   God, the promised (angel—Savior).

3. Gabriel told Mary that the power of the
   Most High would (overshadow—
   overcome) her.

In Words of My Own

1. Why is Mary a special person?

   _____

   _____

   _____

   _____

2. What is unusual about Mary becoming a
   mother?

   _____

   _____

   _____

3. To whom had God promised to send a
   Savior?

   _____

   _____

   _____

   _____

Born of the Virgin Mary.

Words to Use

census

hometown

inn

angels

shepherds

1. People were required to return to their

   family's _____.

2. Family members traveled to take part in a

   _____.

3. The _____ had no room for more

   travelers.

4. Outside Bethlehem, _____

   watched their flocks.

5. _____ were the first to announce

   the Savior's birth.

According to God's Word

1. (Caesar—Marcus) Augustus took a census.

2. Mary traveled to Bethlehem with (David—

   Joseph).

3. Mary laid Jesus in a (manger—basket).

4. The shepherds (hurried—worried) as they

   went to Bethlehem.

5. The shepherds told everyone the (good—

   sad) news.

In Words of My Own

1. What does the news of the angels and

   shepherds mean to you?

   _____

   _____

2. Why is it important to share the good

   news of the coming of the Savior?

   _____

   _____

   _____

   _____

Suffered under Pontius Pilate.

Words to Use

dressed

mocked

whipped

yelled

slapped

twisted

1. At Pilate's order, the soldiers

   _____ Jesus.

2. They _____ together a crown

   of thorns and placed it on Jesus' head.

3. They _____ Jesus, making fun

   of Him.

4. Then they _____ Jesus in a pur-

   ple robe.

5. They _____ Jesus in His face.

6. "Crucify Him!" they _____.

According to God's Word

1. Jesus (suffered—mocked) because of our

   sins.

2. (Julius—Pontius) Pilate was the governor

   before whom Jesus stood trial.

3. The soldiers made fun of Jesus by calling

   Him the (curse—king) of the Jews.

4. Pilate said, "I find no basis for a (charge

   against—release of) Him."

5. Jesus endured pain and suffering because

   He (envies—loves) you and me.

In Words of My Own

1. What did Jesus endure because of our

   sins?

   _____

   _____

2. Describe Jesus' suffering under Pilate.

   _____

   _____

   _____

   _____

   _____

3. How do we know that Jesus cares about

   us?

   _____

   _____

   _____

   _____

Was Crucified.

Words to Use

outside

committed

bowed

into

next to

forgave

asked

1. After nailing Jesus to the cross, the soldiers placed it _____ the ground.

2. Jesus forgave the criminal being crucified _____ Him.

3. Jesus _____ those who were crucifying Him.

4. Jesus _____ John to care for His mother.

5. Jesus _____ His Spirit to God.

6. Jesus finally _____ His head and died for the sins of the world.

According to God's Word

1. Jesus carried his own (cross—drink) to Golgotha.

2. Jesus spoke of God (forsaking —forgiving) Him because of our sins.

3. From the cross Jesus said, "It is (criminal—finished)."

In Words of My Own

1. What is truly amazing about Jesus' forgiveness?

_____

_____

_____

2. How did Jesus show Himself to be God while dying on the cross?

_____

_____

3. How did Jesus show Himself to be human while dying on the cross?

_____

_____

_____

4. For whose sins did Jesus suffer and die?

_____

_____

_____

Died and Was Buried.

Words to Use

Arimathea

spices

Pilate

crucifixion

tomb

1. Joseph was from _____.

2. Joseph and Nicodemus received permission from _____.

3. Joseph and Nicodemus wrapped Jesus' body together with _____.

4. They place Jesus in a _____.

5. Jesus was buried near the site of His _____.

According to God's Word

1. (Friends—enemies) of Jesus asked for His body.

2. They rolled a (log—stone) against the entrance to the grave.

3. After burying Jesus, Joseph and Nicodemus went to their (church—homes).

In Words of My Own

1. How do we know that Jesus was truly dead?

_____

_____

_____

2. How do we know that Pilate believed Jesus was really dead?

_____

_____

_____

3. Tell what we know from God's Word about Jesus' tomb.

_____

_____

_____

_____

He descended into hell.
The third day He rose again from the dead.

Words to Use

proclaim
rose
rolled
reserved
filled

1. Hell is _____ for the devil and those without faith in Jesus.

2. Jesus went to hell to _____ His victory.

3. Jesus _____ again from the dead.

4. The angel _____ the stone away from the entrance to Jesus' tomb.

5. The women were _____ with joy at the angel's news.

According to God's Word

1. After His (death—resurrection) Jesus went to preach to those in hell.

2. Early on Easter morning there was a violent (earthquake—murder).

3. The angel came from (heaven—hell) to Jesus' tomb.

4. The women hurried (to—away from) the tomb after hearing the angel's news.

In Words of My Own

1. Why were the women happy after hearing the angel's news?

_____

_____

_____

2. Why do you think the women were in a hurry after hearing the angel's news?

_____

_____

_____

3. What does Jesus' resurrection mean to you?

_____

_____

_____

_____

He ascended into heaven and sits at the right hand of God, the Father Almighty.

Words to Use

forty

two

one

left

right

1. After His resurrection Jesus spent _____ days appearing to many people.

2. Jesus _____ His disciples to go to His Father in heaven.

3. Suddenly _____ angels appeared.

4. _____ day Jesus will return.

5. Now Jesus is in heaven at His Father's _____ hand.

According to God's Word

1. Jesus led His disciples to a place near (Jerusalem—Bethany).

2. Here Jesus rose from the (ground—dead).

3. A cloud (covered—lifted) Jesus.

4. As Jesus ascended He (rebuked—blessed) the disciples.

5. The Bible says that Jesus will come again (eventually—soon).

In Words of My Own

1. Why did Jesus appear to many after His resurrection?

_____

_____

_____

_____

_____

2. For what purpose will Jesus come back?

_____

_____

_____

_____

From thence He will come to judge the living and the dead.

Words to Use

know

promise

judge

live

go

1. God keeps every _____.

2. From God's Word we _____ that Jesus will come again.

3. Jesus will come again to_____ all people.

4. Those who do not believe will _____ to eternal punishment.

5. Those who believe will _____ with Jesus forever.

According to God's Word

1. All (believers—people) will see Jesus and recognize Him as God's Son and the Savior of the world.

2. (Believers—Unbelievers) will go to eternal punishment in hell.

3. In hell will be the devil and the evil (believers—angels).

4. Jesus promises the (happiness—struggles) of heaven to those with faith.

In Words of My Own

1. How does heaven differ from hell?

_____

_____

_____

_____

_____

2. How do people who will go to heaven differ from those who will go to hell?

_____

_____

_____

3. Why do you believe you will one day go to heaven?

_____

_____

_____

_____

The Third Article

Sanctification

Words to Use

raise

sanctifies

calls

enlightens

forgives

1. The Holy Spirit _____ us by the Gospel.

2. The Holy Spirit _____ believers with His gifts.

3. The Holy Spirit _____ believers and keeps us in the true faith.

4. The Holy Spirit _____ all our sins and the sins of all believers.

5. One day the Holy Spirit will _____ us from the dead.

According to God's Word

1. I (can—cannot) believe in Jesus by my own reason or strength.

2. The Holy Spirit calls, (gathers—dispels), enlightens, and sanctifies us.

3. The Holy Spirit keep us in the one true (faith—translation).

4. He (daily—poorly) and richly forgives the sins of all believers.

5. On the Last Day He will (raise—condemn) me and all the dead.

In Words of My Own

1. How do you know that the Holy Spirit has been at work in your life?

_____

_____

_____

_____

_____

_____

2. What did the Holy Spirit do for you through the Gospel?

_____

_____

_____

I believe in the Holy Spirit, the holy Christian church, the communion of saints.

Words to Use

fire
Baptism
fifty
3,000
wind

1. The Holy Spirit came upon God's people _____ days after Easter.

2. At the coming of the Holy Spirit the people heard a sound like a mighty _____.

3. Then what appeared to be tongues of _____ separated and appeared on Jesus' followers.

4. Peter preached about Jesus. He spoke about repentance and _____.

5. About _____ people became believers on that day.

According to God's Word

1. The Holy Spirit came upon Jesus' followers at the feast of (Pentecost—Purim).

2. God's people began to (speak—sing) in languages they had not learned.

3. Peter (preached—opposed) a powerful sermon about Jesus.

4. By the power of the Holy Spirit at work through Word and Sacraments, the Christian (church—town) grew.

5. Believers often came (together—away) to learn, pray, support, and encourage one another.

In Words of My Own

1. What work does the Holy Spirit do through Baptism?

_____

_____

_____

2. What benefits does the Holy Spirit bring through the church?

_____

_____

_____

_____

_____

The forgiveness of sins.

Words to Use

inheritance

son

poor

servants

celebration

1. Jesus once told a story about a son who asked for his _____.

2. After he had wasted the money, the son became very _____.

3. Then the son remembered how well his father's _____ lived.

4. When the son returned, the father welcomed him with gifts and a lavish _____.

5. The forgiving father in the story reminds us of Jesus; the _____ in the story reminds us of ourselves.

According to God's Word

1. The son wasted his money on (parties—charity).

2. The son was so poor that he worked feeding (homeless people—pigs).

3. The father welcomed the young man as a (son—servant).

4. Jesus welcomes us with abundant (grace—things) when we come to Him asking for forgiveness.

In Words of My Own

1. What words from the story tell you that the young man was sorry for what he had done, rather than simply sorry he had run out of money?

   _____

   _____

   _____

2. How did the father show the great love he had for his son?

   _____

   _____

   _____

3. In what ways does Jesus show His great love for you?

   _____

   _____

   _____

   _____

   _____

The resurrection of the body, and the life everlasting. Amen.

Words to Use

change
heaven
death
life
eyes

1. One day the Holy Spirit will bring to

   _____ all who have ever lived.

2. Our _____ will look on Jesus.

3. Jesus will _____ those who believe

   in Him.

4. Those who believe will go from

   _____ to new life.

5. We will live with Jesus in the joy and hap-

   piness of _____.

According to God's Word

1. On the Last Day (even—only) those who

   have been dead for many years will see

   Jesus.

2. Those who believe in Jesus will have glori-

   fied (bodies—deaths).

3. A (butterfly—crown) reminds us of the

   new life we will have after we have been

   changed.

4. A (butterfly—crown) reminds us of the joy

   and happiness Jesus will give us in heaven.

In Words of My Own

1. Why will you be among those who receive
   a glorified body?

   _____

   _____

   _____

   _____

2. Describe heaven.

   _____

   _____

   _____

   _____

   _____

3. Why will you one day be in heaven?

   _____

   _____

   _____

   _____

   _____

The Lord's Prayer

Words to Use

feed

taught

pray

thanks

1. Jesus _____ by what He said and by what He did.

2. Jesus' disciples once asked Him to teach them to _____.

3. Jesus once gave _____ before using His divine power.

4. Jesus used His divine power to _____ thousands.

According to God's Word

1. Jesus taught His (enemies—disciples) to pray.

2. Jesus taught them to pray (the Lord's Prayer—the Apostles' Creed).

3. Jesus looked up to (heaven—the temple) to give thanks.

4. Jesus prayed to His (Mother—Father).

5. Jesus' act of providing food for thousands was a (miracle—mistake).

6. Jesus (broke—gathered) the loaves after He gave thanks.

In Words of My Own

1. For what purpose did Jesus pray before He fed the thousands of people?

_____

_____

2. For what purposes do you pray?

_____

_____

_____

_____

3. Why is the prayer the disciples learned called the Lord's Prayer?

_____

_____

4. What things have you learned about Jesus from what He said and did?

_____

_____

_____

The Introduction

Our Father, who art in heaven.

Words to Use

gifts

earth

penalty

best

heaven

1. We have a Father in _____.

2. God sent His only Son to _____.

3. Our heavenly Father wants those things that are _____ for us.

4. Jesus took the _____ we deserve.

5. Our heavenly Father gives good _____ to us.

According to God's Word

1. We have a heavenly Father who (loves—ignores) us.

2. Jesus took the punishment we (deserved—received).

3. God's (Word—creation) asks, "Which of you, if his son asks for bread, will give him a stone?"

4. Our heavenly Father gives good gifts to those who (ask—tell) Him.

In Words of My Own

1. What kind of things does your Father in heaven desire for you?

   _____

   _____

2. According to God's Word, what will God do for those who ask?

   _____

   _____

   _____

3. How do you know your Father in heaven loves you?

   _____

   _____

   _____

   _____

   _____

The Introduction

What does this mean?

Words to Use

confident

compassion

call

come

children

1. God invites us to _____ Him our Father.

2. God invites us to _____ to Him in prayer.

3. God invites us to be _____ of His care for us.

4. God has _____ on His children.

5. God has made us His _____ because of His great love for us.

According to God's Word

1. Jesus (taught—warned) His followers about His Father's love for all people.

2. The Lord has compassion on those who (fear—scare) Him.

3. "How great is the love the Father has lavished on us, that we should be called children of God," wrote the Apostle (James—John).

In Words of My Own

1. Compare the love of our heavenly Father and that of the best of earthly fathers.

_____

_____

_____

_____

2. In what aspect of our life does God invite His children to be bold?

_____

_____

_____

_____

Due Oct 6   pages 46-47 this book
AND
pages 56-57

The First Petition

Hallowed be Thy name.

Words to Use

bright
John
holiness
listen
prophets

1. Jesus took Peter, James, and _____ to a high mountain.

2. The disciples got a glimpse of the _____ of God.

3. Jesus' face and clothes became very _____.

4. Old Testament _____ appeared.

5. Then God Himself spoke, identifying Jesus as His Son and telling the disciples to _____ to Him.

According to God's Word

1. On the mountain, the Old Testament figures Moses and (Aaron—Elijah) appeared with Jesus.

2. These Old Testament figures talked with Jesus about the (salvation—trouble) He would bring to the world.

3. Then God Himself spoke from (heaven—Jerusalem).

In Words of My Own

1. Describe Jesus' appearance on the mountain.

_____
_____
_____
_____
_____
_____

2. For what reasons was God pleased with His Son Jesus?

_____
_____
_____
_____
_____

The First Petition

What does this mean?

How is God's name kept holy?

Words to Use

kingdom
purity
protect
worry
lives
profanes

1. God's name is kept holy when His Word is taught in truth and _____.

2. God's name is kept holy when God's children lead holy _____ according to God's Word.

3. Anyone who teaches and lives contrary to God's Word _____ the name of God.

4. We ask God to _____ us from misusing His name.

5. Jesus told His followers not to _____.

6. Jesus told His followers to seek God's _____ and His righteousness.

According to God's Word

1. Jesus taught His (angels—disciples) many things about God and His love.

2. "Look at the (birds—butterflies)," Jesus said.

3. Jesus said that birds know your heavenly Father (loves—feeds) them.

4. "Or, why worry about what you are going to (do—wear)," Jesus said.

5. "Look at the (lilies—violets) of the field. They don't care about clothes," Jesus said.

In Words of My Own

1. According to Jesus' teaching, how do God's children live so as to keep God's name holy?

   _____

   _____

   _____

   _____

2. For what reason are God's children not to worry?

   _____

   _____

   _____

   _____

The Second Petition

Thy kingdom come.

Words to Use

favoritism
kingdom
Gentiles
associate

1. Long ago, God's people did not _____ with people who were different from them.

2. God directed Peter to bring the Good News to the _____.

3. Peter said, "Now I know that God does not show _____."

4. Peter helped bring God's _____ to many people.

According to God's Word

1. Long ago, God's people did not interact with those of other (countries—cultures).

2. One day a group of men came to invite Peter to go with them to their (home-town—commander), Caesarea.

3. Peter went (around—with) them.

4. Peter told the Gentiles that Jesus died to take away (Jewish—their) sins.

In Words of My Own

1. What do we pray according to the Second Petition?

_____

_____

_____

2. Why does Jesus want His followers to help extend His kingdom?

_____

_____

_____

_____

_____

_____

The Second Petition

What does this mean?

How does God's kingdom come?

Words to Use

holy Word
Holy Spirit
come
itself
godly

1. God's kingdom comes by _____.

2. We pray that it will _____ to us also.

3. God's kingdom comes when God gives us the _____ _____.

4. The Holy Spirit makes it possible for us to believe His _____ _____.

5. The Holy Spirit helps us to lead a _____ life.

According to God's Word

1. Paul and his friend (Peter—Silas) once crossed the (city—sea) to bring the Good News of Jesus to the people living there.

2. Outside Philippi they met a (business-woman—housewife) named Lydia.

3. The Lord (opened—hardened) Lydia's heart, and she became a believer.

4. Lydia and her (employers—family) were baptized.

5. Lydia invited Paul and his friend to stay in her (town—house).

In Words of My Own

1. How did God's kingdom come to Lydia?

_____

_____

_____

_____

2. How did you receive God's kingdom?

_____

_____

_____

_____

_____

_____

The Third Petition

Thy will be done on earth as it is in heaven.

Words to Use

prayed

will

cup

angel

night

1. Jesus went to Gethsemane the _____ before His death.

2. Jesus _____ to His Father.

3. Jesus asked His Father to take away the _____ of His suffering.

4. Jesus asked that His Father's _____ be done.

5. God sent an _____ to give Jesus strength.

According to God's Word

1. Jesus went to the (Garden—Rock) of Gethsemane.

2. Here Jesus prayed the same prayer (three—twelve) times.

3. In the Third Petition we ask that God's will be done on (heaven—earth).

In Words of My Own

1. How did Jesus pray regarding God's will?

   _____

   _____

   _____

   _____

2. What was the Father's will regarding Jesus' payment for our sins?

   _____

   _____

   _____

   _____

The Third Petition

What does this mean?

How is God's will done?

Words to Use

hallow
will
come
world
enemy
telling
persecute

1. God's _____ is good and gracious.

2. God's will is done when His people _____ His name.

3. God's will is done when those forces are held in check that do not want to let God's kingdom _____.

4. The devil, the _____, and our sinful nature have an evil plan and purpose with regard to God's will.

5. At first Paul was an _____ of the people of God.

6. But Jesus appeared to Paul and asked Paul, "Why do you _____ Me?"

7. God's will for Paul's life was to travel the world, _____ people about Jesus.

According to God's Word

1. God's will is done when He strengthens us and keeps us firm in the faith until we (die—sin).

2. Saul threatened to kill the (enemies—followers) of Jesus.

3. Saul was on his way to (reward—capture) Christians in Damascus.

4. After Jesus spoke to Saul on the road, Saul became a Christian (persecutor—himself).

5. Saul was baptized and became a (soldier—missionary) named Paul.

In Words of My Own

1. What was God's will for Paul?

   _____

   _____

   _____

   _____

2. What is God's will for you and for all people?

   _____

   _____

   _____

   _____

The Fourth Petition

Give us this day our daily bread.

Words to Use

Savior
live
work
blessings
friends

1. God gives us everything we need to

   _____ .

2. In the Fourth Petition we thank God for

   His many _____

3. We thank God for giving us meaningful

   _____ to do.

4. We thank God for giving us good

   _____ with whom we can share our

   joys and sorrows.

5. Jesus is not only our _____; He is

   our best and truest friend.

According to God's Word

1. In addition to food and clothes, God also
   gave Paul good (spouses—friends).

2. Paul's friends Priscilla and Aquila spent
   time with Paul making (tents—clothes).

3. As Paul and his friends worked together,
   they talked about (Jesus—camping).

In Words of My Own

1. What blessings has God given you to
   make your life comfortable and enjoyable?

   _____

   _____

   _____

   _____

2. Why is Jesus God's best gift to you?

   _____

   _____

   _____

   _____

The Fourth Petition

What does this mean?

What is meant by daily bread?

Words to Use

everything

prayers

thanksgiving

men

daily

1. God gives _____ bread to everyone.

2. In the Fourth Petition we ask God to help us to realize His goodness to us and to help us receive our blessings with _____.

3. God continues to bless us even without our _____.

4. Daily bread includes _____ that has to do with the support and needs of the body.

5. Jesus told His disciples, "From now on you will catch _____."

According to God's Word

1. God gives daily bread also to those who are (dead—evil).

2. Jesus did a miracle before He (called—denounced) His first disciples.

3. The miracle involved their (work—hobby) of fishing.

4. When the disciples did as Jesus asked, they caught so many fish their (hearts—nets) began to break.

In Words of My Own

1. Why does God give good things to all people?

   _____

   _____

2. What did Jesus' words to His disciples "about catching men" mean?

   _____

   _____

   _____

   _____

3. What did the disciples leave behind to follow Jesus?

   _____

   _____

   _____

The Fifth Petition

And forgive us our trespasses as we forgive those who trespass against us.

Words to Use

perfume

tears

hair

guest

trespasses

1. In the Fifth Petition we pray that God will forgive our sins, or _____.

2. Jesus was once a _____ in someone's house.

3. A woman washed Jesus' feet with her _____.

4. She dried Jesus' feet with her _____.

5. Then she poured _____ on Jesus' feet.

According to God's Word

1. The woman washed Jesus' feet at (dinner—breakfast).

2. The woman had lived a (holy—sinful) life.

3. The woman came up to Jesus and began to (cry—speak).

4. The woman (powdered—kissed) Jesus' feet.

5. Jesus (scolded—forgave) the woman.

6. Jesus told the woman, "Your (worship—faith) has saved you; go in peace."

In Words of My Own

1. Why did the woman treat Jesus as she did?

_____

_____

_____

2. What do Jesus' actions tell us about Him?

_____

_____

_____

_____

_____

3. Why could the woman now be at peace?

_____

_____

_____

The Fifth Petition

What does this mean?

Words to Use

worthy

sins

grace

limits

punishment

1. We pray in the Fifth Petition that our Father in heaven would not deny our prayer because of our _____.

2. We are not _____ of the things for which we pray.

3. We ask that God would give to us the things we ask for because of His _____.

4. Because we are sinners, we deserve only God's _____.

5. God's forgiveness for us in Christ Jesus knows no _____.

According to God's Word

1. Peter once asked Jesus if he should forgive someone up to (seven—seventy-seven) times.

2. Jesus told Peter he should forgive someone (seven—seventy-seven) times.

3. Once Jesus forgave Peter for denying (Him—his prayer).

4. No sin is too (great—holy) for God to forgive.

In Words of My Own

1. What message did Jesus give when He told Peter to forgive up to seventy-seven times?

   _____

   _____

   _____

2. For what reason do believers in Jesus forgive others?

   _____

   _____

   _____

3. Describe the kind of forgiveness Jesus gives you.

   _____

   _____

   _____

   _____

The Sixth Petition

And lead us not into temptation.

Words to Use

swear

wept

servant

proclaim

waited

1. Peter was bold enough to _____ that He would never disown Jesus.

2. Peter _____ in the courtyard for news of Jesus' trial.

3. The girl who pointed out Peter as a follower of Jesus was a _____.

4. As Peter denied knowing Jesus, he began to curse and _____.

5. Realizing what he had done, Peter went outside and _____.

According to God's Word

1. On the (morning—night) of Jesus' arrest, Peter declared that he would never disown Jesus.

2. Later that (morning—night) Peter awaited news of Jesus' trial.

3. Peter denied knowing Jesus with an (oath—apology).

4. Peter remembered the (blessing—warning) Jesus had given him.

5. After denying Jesus the third time, Peter (realized—repeated) what he had done.

In Words of My Own

1. How do we know that Peter was sorry for denying Jesus?

   _____

   _____

   _____

   _____

2. How do we know that Jesus was willing to forgive Peter?

   _____

   _____

   _____

   _____

The Sixth Petition

What does this mean?

Words to Use

God

Uz

devil

Satan

Job

1. _____ tempts no one.

2. Together with the world and our sinful flesh, the _____ attacks us regularly.

3. _____ was a faithful follower of the true God.

4. Another name for the devil is _____.

5. Job lived in _____.

According to God's Word

1. Giving in to temptation leads to false belief, despair, and other great shame and (vice—victory).

2. We pray in the Sixth Petition that we will (overlook—overcome) temptation.

3. Satan brought Job (torments—toys).

4. Job was covered with (dust—boils) from head to foot.

5. Job (cursed—trusted) God.

6. (God—Satan) helped Job resist temptation.

In Words of My Own

1. When will all believers finally win victory and no longer be tempted?

   _____

   _____

   _____

   _____

2. How did Job regard God as he endured his suffering?

   _____

   _____

3. What can we learn about God from the story of Job?

   _____

   _____

   _____

   _____

   _____

The Seventh Petition

But deliver us from evil.

Words to Use

give

eat

protect

deliver

beg

1. A woman came to Jesus to _____ Him to heal her daughter.

2. "It is not right to _____ the children's food to the dogs," Jesus said.

3. The woman agreed with Jesus, but she replied that dogs do sometimes _____ food that falls from the master's table.

4. God wants us to ask Him to _____ us.

5. In the Seventh Petition, we ask God to _____ us from pain, harm, and dangers.

According to God's Word

1. Once a (Levite—Canaanite) woman came to Jesus.

2. The woman didn't (give—speak) up asking Jesus to help her.

3. Jesus (granted—rebuffed) the woman's request.

4. "Your faith is (weak—great)!" Jesus said.

5. God has all the (time—power) to help us in the way He knows is best.

In Words of My Own

1. What does Jesus teach us to ask of God in the words of the Seventh Petition?

   _____

   _____

   _____

   _____

   _____

2. What can we learn from the woman about prayer?

   _____

   _____

   _____

   _____

   _____

The Seventh Petition

What does this mean?

Words to Use

rescue

summary

sorrow

evil

hour

1. We offer the Seventh Petition, the last petition in the prayer, in _____.

2. In the Seventh Petition, we ask God to _____ us.

3. We ask for deliverance from every _____.

4. We ask God for a blessed end when our last _____ comes.

5. Luther calls this world a valley of _____.

According to God's Word

1. (Jesus—Lazarus) once told a story of a rich man and a poor man.

2 When both men died, angels carried the (rich—poor) man to heaven.

3. The (rich—poor) man went to hell.

4. The (rich—poor) man had faith.

5. People are taken to heaven on account of their (faith in Jesus—many good works).

In Words of My Own

1. Why did the rich man go to hell while the poor man went to heaven?

_____

_____

_____

_____

_____

2. From what evil is everyone delivered who trusts in Jesus as his or her Savior?

_____

_____

_____

_____

_____

The Conclusion

For Thine is the kingdom and the power and the glory forever and ever.* Amen.

What does this mean?

Words to Use

glorify

heard

commanded

promised

pleasing

1. We can be certain that the petitions we pray are _____ to God.

2. God has _____ us to pray.

3. We can be certain that our petitions are _____ by God.

4. God _____ to hear our prayers.

5. Angels in heaven _____ God.

According to God's Word

1. (Amen—Alleluia) means, "Yes, yes, it shall be so."

2. The Apostle John wrote by (inspiration—rejection) of the Holy Spirit.

3. John describes thousands of angels praising God for the (salvation—wealth) He brings to God's people.

4. Jesus is the victorious (Lamb—Angel) of God.

In Words of My Own

1. Describe God's heavenly kingdom.

_____

_____

_____

_____

_____

_____

2. Why is Jesus worthy to receive power and wealth and wisdom and strength and honor and glory and praise?

_____

_____

_____

_____

3. What victory did Jesus win for us?

_____

_____

_____

*These words were not in Luther's Small Catechism.

The Sacrament of Holy Baptism

Holy Baptism

Words to Use

faith

family

Spirit

gift

body

1. God gives Baptism as a _____ to His people.

2. We receive God's blessings by _____ through Baptism.

3. In Baptism each of us becomes a member of the _____ of God.

4. We are all baptized by one _____.

5. We are all baptized into one _____.

According to God's Word

1. God's Word teaches us to baptize in the (place—name) of the Father and of the Son and of the Holy Spirit.

2. In Baptism, God works forgiveness of sins, new life, and (standards—salvation).

3. The body into which believers are baptized is (united in—divided by) Christ.

In Words of My Own

1. What gifts are received in Baptism?

_____

_____

_____

_____

_____

2. What does it mean to be a member of the family of God through faith in Christ Jesus?

_____

_____

_____

_____

_____

Holy Baptism: First Section

What is Baptism?

Words to Use

Galilee

Jordan

heaven

dove

water

1. Baptism combines God's Word with

   _____.

2. Jesus came from _____ to be baptized by John.

3. Jesus came to the _____ River to be baptized by John.

4. The Holy Spirit came down like a

   _____.

5. God the Father spoke from _____.

According to God's Word

1. Baptism (is—is not) just plain water.

2. As soon as Jesus was baptized, He came out of (Galilee—the water).

3. (Heaven—The river) opened after Jesus was baptized.

3. The Holy Spirit (landed—frowned) upon Jesus.

4. "This is My (Son—dove), whom I love," said God the Father.

5. "With Him I am well (pleased—thanked)," said God the Father.

In Words of My Own

1. What makes simple water into Baptism?

   _____

   _____

   _____

   _____

2. Identify the Father, Son, and Holy Spirit at Jesus' Baptism.

   _____

   _____

   _____

   _____

   _____

   _____

   _____

Holy Baptism: First Section

Which is that word of God?

Words to Use

> earth
> nations
> disciples
> resurrection
> mountain

1. After His _____ Jesus gathered His followers together.

2. Jesus' _____ worshiped Him in the region of Galilee.

3. Jesus spoke to His followers on a _____ in Galilee.

4. Jesus told them to make disciples of all _____.

5. Jesus told His followers to bring the Good News to everyone on _____.

According to God's Word

1. Jesus said, "All authority in heaven and on earth has been (given to—taken from) Me."

2. Jesus told His followers to baptize in the (place—name) of the Father and of the Son and of the Holy Spirit.

3. Jesus told His followers to teach people to (obey—ignore) everything He had commanded.

4. Jesus promised to (be with—send forth) His followers to the very end of the age.

5. These words of Jesus, also called the Great Commission, are recorded in the last chapter of (Matthew—Mark).

In Words of My Own

1. What words of God are Christians to use to baptize people?

   _____

   _____

   _____

   _____

   _____

2. What comforting assurance do God's people have as they share the Gospel?

   _____

   _____

   _____

   _____

   _____

Holy Baptism: Second Section

What benefits does Baptism give?

Words to Use

belongs

rescues

gives

works

promises

1. Baptism _____ forgiveness of sins.

2. Baptism _____ from death and the devil.

3. Baptism _____ eternal salvation to all who believe.

3. The words and _____ of God tell us of the benefits of Baptism.

4. Referring to children, Jesus said, "The kingdom of God _____ to such as these."

According to God's Word

1. (People—The disciples) were bringing little children to Jesus.

2. (Jesus—The disciples) tried to keep the children away.

3. Jesus was not pleased with the (children—disciples).

4. "Let the (children—disciples) come to Me," Jesus said, "and do not hinder them."

In Words of My Own

1. How does Jesus feel towards children?

_____

_____

_____

_____

2. What blessings has Jesus given you through Baptism?

_____

_____

_____

_____

_____

_____

Holy Baptism: Second Section

Which are these words and promises of God?

Words to Use

traveled

saved

told

baptized

condemned

died

1. Whoever believes and is baptized will be

   _____.

2. Whoever does not believe will be

   _____.

3. Philip met a man as he _____.

4. Philip_____ the man about Jesus.

5. Philip explained that Jesus _____

   for the sins of the world.

6. Philip _____the man.

According to God's Word

1. The man was an official in (pursuit—charge) of the treasury of Candace.

2. Candace was the queen of (Ethiopia—Isaiah).

3. The man was reading about a (lamb—bull) that was killed.

4. Philip told the man about how Jesus is the (Savior—ruler) of the world.

5. The man (rejoiced—rested) after being baptized.

In Words of My Own

1. What did the man from Ethiopia ask after he came to believe in Jesus?

   _____

   _____

2. Why did the man act as he did after being baptized?

   _____

   _____

   _____

   _____

3. What words and promises of God are associated with Baptism?

   _____

   _____

   _____

   _____

Holy Baptism: Third Section

How can water do such great things?

Words to Use

grace

plain

faith

rebirth

heirs

1. Without God's Word water is _____ water and no Baptism.

2. Water does great things in Baptism because it is connected with God's Word and _____ that trusts God's Word.

3. With the Word of God present there is a Baptism, that is, a life-giving water rich in _____.

4. God saved us through the washing of _____ and renewal by the Holy Spirit.

5. Having been justified by His grace, we become _____ who have the hope of eternal life.

According to God's Word

1. Nicodemus was a (Pharisee—Samaritan).

2. Nicodemus came to see Jesus one (morning—night).

3. Jesus told Nicodemus that no one can enter the kingdom of God without first being (baptized—born) again.

4. Jesus told Nicodemus that whoever believes in Him shall not (suffer—perish) but have eternal life.

In Words of My Own

1. How would you answer Nicodemus's question?

   _____

   _____

2. What kind of washing does the Holy Spirit do in Baptism?

   _____

   _____

3. Explain how someone is born again in Jesus.

   _____

   _____

   _____

   _____

   _____

   _____

Holy Baptism: Fourth Section

What does such baptizing with water indicate?

_____

Where is this written?

_____

Words to Use

arise

live

die

buried

1. By daily contrition and repentance our sinful nature should be drowned and _____.

2. Baptism indicates that a new person should daily emerge and _____.

3. We are _____ with Christ through Baptism into death.

4. By remembering our Baptism, we too may _____ a new life.

According to God's Word

1. The Old Adam is our (sinful nature— first parent).

2. In Baptism the new man should arise (daily—at the Last Day).

3. The new life God gives us to live in Him is a life of righteousness and (purity— privacy) forever.

4. Christ was raised from the dead through the glory of (the Father—Baptism).

In Words of My Own

1. What does Baptism mean for the daily life of a Christian?

_____

_____

_____

_____

_____

2. How does God preserve us in our Baptism?

_____

_____

_____

_____

Confession

What is confession?

_____

What sins should we confess?

_____

Words to Use

Pharisee
pastor
forgiveness
absolution
tax collector

1. The two parts of confession include confessing our sins and receiving

   _____.

2. Absolution is received from the

   _____ as from God Himself.

3. _____ is another word for

   absolution.

4. Jesus once told a story about a

   _____ and a tax collector.

5. The sins of the _____ _____

   were forgiven.

According to God's Word

1. Before God we should plead guilty of
   (no—all) sins.

2. We should (confess to—withhold from)
   the pastor those sins that we know and
   feel in our hearts.

3. Jesus told a story about two men who
   went to the (temple—synagogue) to pray.

4. The Pharisee (thanked—blamed) God that
   he was not like other men.

5. The tax collector prayed, "God have
   (mercy on—fear of) me, a sinner."

In Words of My Own

1. From whom does the forgiveness pronounced by the pastor really come?

   _____

   _____

   _____

   _____

2. Why did one man in Jesus' story go home
   with his sins forgiven while the other man
   did not?

   _____

   _____

   _____

   _____

   _____

Confession

Words to Use

praise

Psalms

place

prophet

1. Martin Luther tells us to think about our _____ in life according to the Ten Commandments as we approach confession.

2. Nathan the _____ once talked to David about his sin.

3. David offered thanks and _____ to God for His forgiveness.

4. Many of David's songs are included in the book of _____.

According to God's Word

1. Luther says to ask yourself: "Are you a father, mother, son, daughter, husband, wife, or (worker—traveler)?"

2. Luther says to ask yourself: "Have you been disobedient, unfaithful, or (unhappy—lazy)?"

3. Luther says to ask yourself: "Have you been hot-tempered, (rude—ruthless), or quarrelsome?"

4. Luther says to ask yourself: "Have you (hurt—helped) someone by your words or deeds?"

5. Luther says to ask yourself: "Have you (stolen—saved something), been negligent, wasted anything, or done any harm?"

In Words of My Own

1. How did David feel after receiving assurance that his sins had been taken away?

   _____

   _____

   _____

   _____

   _____

2. How did God take away David's sins and yours?

   _____

   _____

   _____

   _____

A Short Form of Confession

Words to Use

confessor
servant
sinner
master
penitent

1. The person making the confession is referred to as the _____.

2. The person hearing the confession is referred to as the _____.

3. The person making the confession might say, "I, a poor _____, plead guilty before God of all sins."

4. The person making the confession might say, "I, sad to say, serve my _____ unfaithfully, for in this and that I have not done what I was told to do."

5. Jacob once said to God, "I am unworthy of all the kindness and faithfulness You have shown Your _____."

According to God's Word

1. Jacob once reflected on God's grace and (goodness—justice).

2. Jacob once (boldly—humbly) praised God for His mercy and love.

3. Jacob praised God for His kindness and (faithfulness—unfaithfulness).

In Words of My Own

1. What have been the consequences of your sin?

_____

_____

_____

_____

_____

2. What do you believe about all the sins you have asked God to forgive for Jesus' sake?

_____

_____

_____

_____

_____

A Short Form of Confession

Words to Use

set
curse
quarrel
overcharging
speak

1. I commit a sin when I _____ with my friends.

2. Another example of a sin is to _____ at a parent.

3. Parents sin when they _____ a bad example by indecent words and deeds.

4. I sin when I hurt or _____ evil of a neighbor.

5. The storeowner sins by _____, selling inferior merchandise, or giving less than was paid for.

According to God's Word

1. The Bible teaches us that the forgiveness we receive from our confessor is really (God's—false) forgiveness.

2. The words of Jesus recorded in Holy Scripture (command—forbid) believers to forgive one another.

3. The confessor may also (comfort—burden) the penitent with additional passages from God's Word.

In Words of My Own

1. Why can the forgiven Christian "go in peace"?

_____

_____

_____

_____

_____

2. How do we know that God desires to forgive our sins?

_____

_____

_____

The Office of the Keys

What is the Office of the Keys?

_____

Where is this written?

_____

What do you believe according to these words?

_____

Words to Use

Evangelist

valid

Christ

authority

church

1. The Office of the Keys is a special _____ given by Christ to forgive sin.

2. Christ has given the Office of the Keys to His _____ on earth.

3. St. John the _____ recorded that Jesus gave the Office of the Keys to His disciples.

4. When called ministers deal with people according to God's Word, their actions are _____ and certain.

5. When called ministers deal with people according to God's Word, it is as if _____ dealt with them Himself.

According to God's Word

1. The Office of the Keys authorizes the church to (forgive—withhold forgiveness from) repentant sinners.

2. The Office of the Keys authorizes the church to (absolve—exclude) openly unrepentant sinners from the Christian congregation.

3. Jesus gave this Office of the Keys to His disciples on the day of His (Baptism—resurrection).

4. When Jesus appeared to them, the disciples were (angry—overjoyed).

5. Jesus said, "I am (forgiving—sending) you. Receive the Holy Spirit. If you forgive anyone his sins, they are forgiven; if you do not forgive them, they are not forgiven."

In Words of My Own

1. How should a Christian congregation and its members treat openly unrepentant members?

_____

_____

_____

_____

2. How would God have the members of His church regard those who repent of their sins?

_____

_____

_____

_____

The Sacrament of the Altar

Words to Use

proclaim

drink

cup

broke

eat

1. We remember how Jesus gave His body for us when we _____ the bread in the Sacrament of the Altar.

2. We remember how Jesus shed His blood for us when we _____ the wine in the Lord's Supper.

3. When Jesus first gave the Sacrament, He _____ the bread.

4. "This _____ is the new covenant of My blood," Jesus said.

5. According to 1 Corinthians 11:23b-26, believers _____ the Lord's death when they receive the Lord's Supper

According to God's Word

1. Jesus first gave the Lord's Supper on the (morning—night) of His betrayal.

2. Jesus took the bread and then gave (thanks—payment) for the bread.

3. Jesus said, "This is My (body—best)."

4. Jesus took the (cup—candle) and began speaking about His blood.

5. Jesus said, "Do this, whenever you drink it, in (remembrance—fear) of Me."

Words of My Own

1. What two things do believers do, in remembrance of Jesus, in the Sacrament of the Altar?

   _____

   _____

   _____

   _____

2. With regard to the Sacrament of the Altar, what are believers to do until Jesus comes?

   _____

   _____

   _____

   _____

   _____

The Sacrament of The Altar

What is the Sacrament of the Altar?

_____

Where is this written?

_____

Words to Use

poured

during

true

under

instituted

1. In the Sacrament of the Altar participants receive the _____ body and blood of our Lord Jesus Christ.

2. Participants in the Sacrament receive Christ's body and blood _____ the bread and wine.

3. The Sacrament has been _____ by Christ Himself.

4. Jesus gave His disciples the bread _____ the meal.

5. Jesus describes His blood as being _____ out for many for the forgiveness of sins.

According to God's Word

1. The night before His (betrayal—death), Jesus gave His disciples the first Sacrament of the Altar.

2. Jesus shared the (Passover—Baptismal) meal with His disciples.

3 After Jesus took the cup, He gave (suggestions—thanks) and offered it to the disciples.

4. The holy Evangelists Matthew, Mark, and (Luke—John), as well as St. Paul, write about Jesus giving the Sacrament of the Altar.

5. Jesus (shed—shielded) His blood for the forgiveness of our sins.

In Words of My Own

1. To whom does Jesus refer when He says the words "for you"?

_____

_____

_____

_____

2. How do believers receive the Sacrament of the Altar?

_____

_____

_____

_____

_____

The Sacrament of The Altar

What is the benefit of this eating and drinking?

_____

How can bodily eating and drinking do such great things?

_____

Words to Use

drink

shed

given

forgiveness

eat

1. Christ's body was _____ for us for the forgiveness of our sins.

2. Christ's blood was _____ for us for the forgiveness of our sins.

3. Participants in the Sacrament of the Altar receive Christ's body when they _____ the bread.

4. Participants in the Sacrament of the Altar receive Christ's blood when they _____ the wine.

5. Participants in the Sacrament of the Altar receive _____.

According to God's Word

1. Where there is the forgiveness of sins, there is also (life—hope) and salvation.

2. God's words along with the (spiritual—bodily) eating and drinking are the chief things in the Sacrament.

3. Whoever believes Jesus' words has exactly what they say: "(fullness—forgiveness) of sins."

4. "For whenever you eat this bread and drink this cup, you (deny—proclaim) the Lord's death until He comes" (1 Corinthians 11:26).

In Words of My Own

1. In addition to eating and drinking, what is another essential part of the Sacrament of the Altar?

_____

_____

_____

2. Along with forgiveness of sins, what else is received by those who participate in the Sacrament of the Altar?

_____

_____

_____

_____

_____

The Sacrament of The Altar

Who receives this sacrament worthily?

Words to Use

require

fast

spread

cook

prepare

1. To _____ and otherwise prepare to receive the Sacrament of the Altar is fine outward training.

2. The words "for you" _____ all hearts to believe.

3. While they lived in Egypt, God told His people to _____ a special lamb.

4. God's people were to _____ and eat the lamb.

5. God's people _____ the lamb's blood on the doorframe of their homes.

According to God's Word

1. Anyone who does not believe God's words is (unhappy—unworthy) to receive the Sacrament.

2. Anyone who does not believe God's words is (unprepared—unpredictable).

3. On (Passover—Easter) night the angel of the Lord killed the firstborn of every house that did not have blood on the doorframe.

4 (Jesus—Pharaoh) commanded God's people to leave Egypt.

5. God delivers His people from the (slavery—victory) of sin through the blood of Jesus.

In Words of My Own

1. Why should unbelievers not participate in the Sacrament of the Altar?

_____

_____

_____

_____

2. How does the Sacrament of the Altar remind us of the Passover?

_____

_____

_____

_____

_____

Daily Prayers

Morning and Evening Prayer

Words to Use

keep

cross

forgive

name

place

1. Luther suggests that upon rising in the morning and upon going to bed at night believers make the sign of the _____.

2. When we pray in the _____ of the Father and of the Son and of the Holy Spirit, we remember our Baptism.

3. We ask that God will _____ us safe from sin and all evil.

4. In our prayer we _____ ourselves into the hands of God.

5. In the evening prayer we ask God to _____ the sins we have committed.

According to God's Word

1. Luther suggests that at morning and at night Christians repeat the (creed—concordance) and the Lord's Prayer.

2. Both morning and evening prayers begin with an expression of (regret—thanks).

3. In both prayers we ask God to send His holy (apostles—angel) to be with us.

4. In both prayers we ask that the evil (foe—thought) will have no power over us.

In Words of My Own

1. Why can God's people be happy after placing themselves in the hands of God?

_____

_____

_____

_____

2. Why do Christians pray in Jesus' name?

_____

_____

_____

_____

_____

_____

_____

Daily Prayers

Asking a Blessing

Returning Thanks

Words to Use

hope

love

food

bountiful

benefits

1. God gives _____ at the proper time to every living thing.

2. God's _____ endures forever.

3. God provides for us out of His _____ goodness.

4. God delights in those who put their _____ in His unfailing love.

5. God joyfully receives our thanks for all the _____ He provides.

According to God's Word

1. God opens His (hand—mind) and satisfies the desires of every living thing.

2. When Christians pray, Luther suggests that they pray reverently and that they (fold—wash) their hands.

3. God gives food to every (demon—creature).

4. Luther suggests that Christians pray the (Lord's—Sinner's) Prayer before and after eating.

5. The table prayers are directed to God the (Father—Spirit).

In Words of My Own

1. How does God regard those who put their hope in His unfailing love?

_____

_____

_____

_____

2 Why do Christians thank God for the food they eat?

_____

_____

_____

_____

_____

_____

_____

Table of Duties

To Bishops, Pastors, and Preachers

What the Hearers Owe Their Pastors

Words to Use

respect
doctrine
obey
reproach
convert

1. The pastor (overseer) must be an honorable person, above _____.

2. The pastor should manage his family well and see that his children _____.

3. The children of the pastor should show him _____.

4. The pastor should not be a recent _____.

5. The pastor should encourage others by teaching sound _____.

According to God's Word

1. Those who preach the gospel should make their (living—demands) by the gospel.

2. Anyone who receives (instruction—justice) in the word must share all good things with his instructor.

3. Those who preach and teach in the church are worthy of (double—half) honor.

4. God's people are to live at (peace—odds) with one another.

5. God wants His people to obey their leaders so that their work is a (joy—burden).

In Words of My Own

1. What makes the work of a pastor or other workers in the church so special?

_____

_____

_____

_____

2. Summarize how God wants His people to regard those who serve them in His church.

_____

_____

_____

_____

_____

_____

Table of Duties

Of Civil Government

Of Citizens

Words to Use

authorities

elders

rulers

agent

servant

1. Paul reminded the _____ of the church at Ephesus of his ministry among them.

2. God's Word says that everyone must submit himself to the governing _____.

3. Those who do right have nothing to fear from _____.

4. The one in authority is God's _____.

5. A person in authority is an _____ of wrath to bring punishment on the wrongdoers.

According to God's Word

1. Paul told those in Ephesus to turn to God in repentance and to have faith in (Jesus—themselves).

2. After they prayed together, the elders (accompanied—abandoned) Paul to the ship.

3. There is no authority except that which God has (established—forbidden).

4. Do what is right and the one in authority will (commend—apprehend) you.

5. Give to Caesar what is (God's—Caesar's).

In Words of My Own

1. What attitude does God want His children to have toward those in authority?

   _____

   _____

   _____

2. Explain what it means to "give to God what is God's."

   _____

   _____

   _____

   _____

   _____

Table of Duties

To Husbands, To Wives

To Parents, To Children

Words to Use

commend

peaceful

considerate

godliness

enjoy

1. God's Word tells us to pray for those in authority so that we may live _____ and quiet lives.

2. God's Word tells us to pray for those in authority so that we may live in _____ and holiness.

3. Those in authority have the power both to punish and to _____ .

4. Husbands are to be _____ as they live with their wives.

5. Children are to obey their parents to that it may go well with them and that they may _____ long life on the earth.

According to God's Word

1. Timothy's mother, (Lois—Eunice), and his grandmother both loved Jesus.

2. Paul once reminded (Lois—Timothy), "From infancy you have known the holy Scriptures, which are able to make you wise for salvation through faith in Christ Jesus" (2 Timothy 3:15).

3. Husbands are to (worship—love) their wives as Christ loved His church.

4. Wives are to submit to their husbands as to (the Lord—their children).

5. To children God says to "(honor—reject) your father and your mother."

In Words of My Own

1. Why is God's Word so important?

_____

_____

_____

_____

2. Who told you about Jesus and His love for you?

_____

_____

_____

_____

Table of Duties

To Workers of All Kinds

To Employers and Supervisors

To Youth

To Widows

To Everyone

Words to Use

summed

treat

obey

humble

clothe

1. God wants us to _____ our earthly masters.

2. Employers and supervisors are to _____ those over whom they have authority with respect and fear and with sincerity of heart.

3. God opposes the proud but gives grace to the _____.

4. God's Word encourages us to _____ ourselves with humility toward one another.

5. The commandments are _____ up in this one rule: "Love your neighbor as yourself."

According to God's Word

1. We are to obey those in authority not only to win their (favor—obedience) when they are watching.

2. We are to serve wholeheartedly, as if serving the (Lord—employer).

3. There is no (favoritism—fraternizing) with God.

4 The young are to be submissive to those who are (older—sincere).

5. The widow who is left all alone puts her hope in God and (prays—sleeps).

In Words of My Own

1. Describe how God would have us treat those in authority over us?

_____

_____

_____

2. When we know the love of God in Christ Jesus, how will we relate to other people?

_____

_____

_____

_____

Christian Questions with Their Answers

Words to Use

wrath

Gospel

hope

commandments

shed

1. Because I have not kept the

   _____, I know I am

   a sinner.

2. Because I am a sinner, I deserve only God's

   _____ and displeasure.

3. Because of Jesus, I _____ to be saved.

4. Because Jesus died for me and _____

   His blood for me, I trust in Him.

5. Because I believe the holy _____,

   I know that Jesus died for me.

According to God's Word

1. I know I am a sinner because I have not
   (kept—seen) the Ten Commandments.

2. Christ is the (Son—Father) of God.

3. There is (one—three) God(s).

4. God the Father (did—did not) die for me.

5. The (Father—Son) is true God and also
   true man.

In Words of My Own

1. What do you deserve according to God's
   Word?

   _____

   _____

   _____

   _____

   _____

2. What has Christ done to bring you salvation?

   _____

   _____

   _____

   _____

   _____

Christian Questions with Their Answers

Words to Use

drink

remember

eat

love

believe

1. Jesus took bread, gave thanks, broke it, and gave it to the disciples and said, "Take, _____; this is My body, which is given for you."

2. Jesus took the cup, gave thanks, gave it to the disciples, and calling the wine His blood said, "This do, as often as you _____it, in remembrance of Me."

3. Those partaking worthily in the Sacrament _____ that the true body and blood of Christ are in the Sacrament.

4. When we eat and drink in the Sacrament we _____ and proclaim Christ's death and the shedding of His blood.

5. Christ died to make full payment for sin because of His great _____ for His Father and for me and other sinners.

According to God's Word

1. Christians remember and proclaim Christ's death so we may learn to believe that no (creature—God) could make satisfaction for our sins; only Christ could do that.

2. We should encourage one another to receive the Sacrament (frequently—daily).

3. A person who does not feel the need for the Sacrament should (believe—refute) what Scriptures say about our bodies in Galatians 5 and Romans 7.

4. A person who does not feel the need for the Sacrament should look around to see whether he is still in the (war—world).

5. A person who does not feel the need for the Sacrament should also remember the continual lying and murdering influence of the (judge—devil).

In Words of My Own

1. Why is the Sacrament referred to as "no child's play"?

_____

_____

_____

_____

2. Why do you wish to receive the Sacrament?

_____

_____

_____

_____

Books of the Bible

Words to Use

Prophetic

Pentateuch

Poetic

Historical

Epistles

1. The first five books of the Bible are referred to as the _____.

2. The first seventeen books of the Bible are _____ books.

3. Job and Proverbs are examples of _____books.

4. Revelation is a _____ book found in the New Testament.

5. Colossians is one of the _____.

According to God's Word

1. (Ezekiel—Job) is one of the Major Prophets.

2. (Daniel—Joel) is one of the Minor Prophets.

3. (Song of Songs—Malachi) is the last book in the Old Testament.

4. Three epistles included in the Bible were written by (Peter—John).

5. The one historical book found in the New Testament that is not named after the apostle who wrote it is (Acts—Jude).

In Words of My Own

1. Into what two parts is the Bible divided?

_____

_____

_____

2. What is the main message of the Bible?

_____

_____

_____

_____

_____

_____

_____

Creeds and Confessions

Words to Use

Smalcald

Concord

Athanasian

Nicene

Augsburg

1. The _____ Creed is often confessed at celebrations of the Lord's Supper.

2. The _____ Creed is read on Holy Trinity Sunday.

3. The _____ Confession was written by Philip Melanchthon.

4. The _____ Articles summarize Luther's main disagreements with the Roman Church.

5. The Formula of _____, completed in 1577, served to resolve doctrinal differences among Lutherans.

Understanding the Confessions

1. Published in 1580, The Book of (Concord—Faith) is a true and unadulterated statement and exposition of the Word of God.

2. The (Large—Small) Catechism is not made up of questions and answers but presents basic Christian teachings in a form often used in sermons.

3. A well-known statement of faith written by Philip Melanchthon was read before Emperor (Maximilian—Charles V) in Augsburg, Germany, in 1530.

4. (Melanchthon—Luther) wrote a Treatise on the Power and Primacy of the Pope.

5. The Formula of Concord (was—was not) an exposition and defense of previously adopted writings.

In Words of My Own

1. What was Luther's purpose in writing the Small Catechism?

_____

_____

_____

_____

2. What important doctrine makes up half of the Apology of the Augsburg Confession?

_____

_____

_____

_____

_____

The Church Year

Sundays and Major Festivals

Minor Festivals

Words to Use

Ash Wednesday
Nativity
Reformation
Transfiguration
Pentecost

1. Another name for Christmas is the

   _____ of our Lord.

2. The _____ of our

   Lord occurs at the end of the season of

   Epiphany.

3. _____ _____ marks the

   beginning of Lent.

4. The festival of _____ marks

   the end of the Easter Season.

5. _____ Day is October 31.

Understanding the Church Year

1. The Ascension of our Lord is observed during the (Epiphany—Easter) season.

2. The first Sunday after Pentecost honors
   the Holy (Sacraments—Trinity).

3. The Circumcision of Our Lord is observed
   on (New Year's—St. Valentine's) Day.

4. On June 24 the Nativity of John (the Bap-
   tist—the Evangelist) is observed.

5. All Saints' Day is the first of (November—
   December).

In Words of My Own

1. Name the three major times of the church
   year.

   _____

   _____

   _____

2. What difference do you find between the
   major and minor festivals of the church?

   _____

   _____

   _____

   _____

   _____

I Am Jesus' Little Lamb

Words to Use

bids

guides

calls

provides

loves

1. Jesus the Good Shepherd gently _____ me through my life.

2. Jesus _____ for me by meeting my needs.

3. Jesus _____ me every day with the same unending care.

4. Jesus _____ me go to where the quiet waters flow.

5. Jesus _____ me by my name.

According to God's Word

1. Knowing Jesus, I can be (glad—sad) at heart.

2. According to the hymn Jesus is my staff and (stay—way), meaning that He keeps me steady as I journey through life.

3. Jesus leads me into pleasant (pastures — palaces).

4. The third verse of the hymn describes each human life as (short—long).

5. In heaven we will rest in the (place—arms) of Jesus.

In Words of My Own

1. How is Jesus like a Good Shepherd?

_____

_____

_____

_____

_____

2. What does Jesus mean to you as you live your life? As you look forward to eternity?

_____

_____

_____

_____

_____

_____

_____

God's Own Child, I Gladly Say It

Words to Use

release
unraveled
pay
sleep
comfort

1. Because I could not _____ redemption's price, God made the payment Himself.

2. Through Baptism I have _____ from a guilty conscience.

3. Through Baptism the might of Satan is _____.

4. I have lifelong _____ knowing I am baptized into Christ.

5. Because I am baptized into Christ, I can _____ secure, even in my grave.

Understanding Hymns

1. In Baptism God (unites—contends) with me.

2. Because of Jesus I die to (inherit—promote) paradise.

3. Even in death the Christian's (faith—appearance) brightly flashes.

4. While my body rests in the ground, my soul will continue (amazing—praising) God.

5. Through faith in Jesus, I'm a child of (Mary—paradise).

In Words of My Own

1. Describe the blessings that are yours in Baptism.

_____

_____

_____

_____

_____

2. Explain the term "forgiving flood" as used to explain Baptism.

_____

_____

_____

_____

_____

Lord, Help Us Ever to Retain

Words to Use

pray
absolve
faith
Sacrament
truth

1. In the Catechism, Luther taught God's Word of _____.

2. In this hymn we pray that we might turn from sin to God in _____.

3. We ask God to hear us when we _____.

4. We also pray that God would forgive or _____ us of our sin.

5. We conclude the hymn asking God to increase our faith through the _____.

Understanding Hymns

1. Luther wrote the catechism in (sophisticated—simple) style.

2. Luther wrote the catechism to be taught to (patriarchs—youth).

3. Our God is referred to as The (One—Three) in One.

4. We (provide—need) God's help every day.

5. God brings children to Himself through (Baptism—condemnation).

In Words of My Own

1. Why did Martin Luther write the catechism?

_____

_____

_____

2. Summarize the Six Chief Parts of Christian doctrine as explained in this hymn.

_____

_____

_____

_____

_____

_____

_____

_____

_____

_____

_____

Soli Deo Gloria!

The Ten Commandments

The First Commandment

You shall have no other gods. (Exodus 20:3)

The Second Commandment

You shall not misuse the name of the LORD your God. (Exodus 20:7)

The Third Commandment

Remember the Sabbath day by keeping it holy. (Exodus 20:8)

Love your neighbor as yourself. (Matthew 22:39)

The Fourth Commandment

Honor your father and your mother. (Exodus 20:12)

The Fifth Commandment

You shall not murder. (Exodus 20:13)

The Sixth Commandment

You shall not commit adultery. (Exodus 20:14)

The Seventh Commandment

You shall not steal. (Exodus 20:15)

The Eighth Commandment

You shall not give false testimony against your neighbor. (Exodus 20:16)

The Ninth Commandment

You shall not covet your neighbor's house. (Exodus 20:17a)

The Tenth Commandment

You shall not covet your neighbor's wife, or his manservant or maidservant, his ox or donkey, or anything that belongs to your neighbor. (Exodus 20:17b)

The Close of the Commandments

What does God say about all these commandments? He says: "I, the LORD your God, am a jealous God, punishing the children for the sin of the fathers to the third and fourth generation of those who hate Me, but showing love to a thousand generations of those who love Me and keep My commandments." [Ex. 20:5-6]

The Apostles' Creed

I believe in God the Father Almighty, Maker of heaven and earth.

And in Jesus Christ, His only Son, our Lord, who was conceived by the Holy Spirit, born of the Virgin Mary, suffered under Pontius Pilate, was crucified, died and was buried. He descended into hell. The third day He rose again from the dead. He ascended into heaven and sits at the right hand of God, the Father Almighty. From thence He will come to judge the living and the dead.

I believe in the Holy Spirit, the holy Christian church, the communion of saints, the forgiveness of sins, the resurrection of the body, and the life everlasting. Amen.

The Lord's Prayer

Our Father who art in heaven, hallowed be Thy name, Thy kingdom come, Thy will be done on earth as it is in heaven. Give us this day our daily bread; and forgive us our trespasses as we forgive those who trespass against us; and lead us not into temptation, but deliver us from evil. For Thine is the kingdom and the power and the glory forever and ever. Amen.

Baptism

FIRST

What is Baptism?

Baptism is not just plain water, but it is the water included in God's command and combined with God's word.

Which is that word of God?

Christ our Lord says in the last chapter of Matthew: "Therefore go and make disciples of all nations, baptizing them in the name of the Father and of the Son and of the Holy Spirit." [Matt. 28:19]

SECOND

What benefits does Baptism give?

It works forgiveness of sins, rescues from death and the devil, and gives eternal salvation to all who believe this, as the words and promises of God declare.

Which are these words and promises of God?

Christ our Lord says in the last chapter of Mark: "Whoever believes and is baptized will be saved, but whoever does not believe will be condemned." [Mark 16:16]

THIRD

How can water do such great things?

Certainly not just water, but the word of God in and with the water does these things, along with the faith which trusts this word of God in the water. For without God's word the water is plain water and no Baptism. But with the word of God it is a Baptism, that is, a life-giving water, rich in grace, and a washing of the new birth in the Holy Spirit, as St. Paul says in Titus, chapter three:

"He saved us through the washing of rebirth and renewal by the Holy Spirit, whom He poured out on us generously through Jesus Christ our Savior, so that, having been justified by His grace, we might become heirs having the hope of eternal life. This is a trustworthy saying." [Titus 3:5-8]

FOURTH

What does such baptizing with water indicate?

It indicates that the Old Adam in us should by daily contrition and repentance be drowned and die with all sins and evil desires, and that a new man should daily emerge and arise to live before God in righteousness and purity forever.

Where is this written?

St. Paul writes in Romans chapter six: "We were therefore buried with Him through baptism into death in order that, just as Christ was raised from the dead through the glory of the Father, we too may live a new life." [Rom. 6:4]

Confession

What is confession?

Confession has two parts.

First, that we confess our sins, and

second, that we receive absolution, that is, forgiveness, from the pastor as from God Himself, not doubting, but firmly believing that by it our sins are forgiven before God in heaven.

What sins should we confess?

Before God we should plead guilty of all sins, even those we are not aware of, as we do in the Lord's Prayer; but before the pastor we should confess only those sins which we know and feel in our hearts.

Which are these?

Consider your place in life according to the Ten Commandments: Are you a father, mother, son, daughter, husband, wife, or worker? Have you been disobedient, unfaithful, or lazy? Have you been hot-tempered, rude, or quarrelsome? Have you hurt someone by your words or deeds? Have you stolen, been negligent, wasted anything, or done any harm?

The Office of the Keys

*What is the Office of the Keys?**

The Office of the Keys is that special authority which Christ has given to His church on earth to forgive the sins of repentant sinners, but to withhold forgiveness from the unrepentant as long as they do not repent.

*Where is this written?**

This is what St. John the Evangelist writes in chapter twenty: The Lord Jesus breathed on His disciples and said, "Receive the Holy Spirit. If you forgive anyone his sins, they are forgiven; if you do not forgive them, they are not forgiven." [John 20:22-23]

*What do you believe according to these words?**

I believe that when the called ministers of Christ deal with us by His divine command, in particular when they exclude openly unrepentant sinners from the Christian congregation and absolve those who repent of their sins and want to do better, this is just as valid and certain, even in heaven, as if Christ our dear Lord dealt with us Himself.

*This question may not have been composed by Luther himself but reflects his teaching and was included in editions of the catechism during his lifetime.

The Sacrament of the Altar

What is the Sacrament of the Altar?

It is the true body and blood of our Lord Jesus Christ under the bread and wine, instituted by Christ himself for us Christians to eat and to drink.

Where is this written?

The holy Evangelists Matthew, Mark, Luke, and St. Paul write:

Our Lord Jesus Christ, on the night when He was betrayed, took bread, and when He had given thanks, He broke it and gave it to the disciples and said: "Take, eat; this is My body, which is given for you. This do in remembrance of Me."

In the same way also He took the cup after supper, and when He had given thanks, He gave it to them, saying, "Drink of it, all of you; this cup is the new testament in My blood, which is shed for you for the forgiveness of sins. This do, as often as you drink it, in remembrance of Me."

What is the benefit of this eating and drinking?

These words, "Given and shed for you for the forgiveness of sins," show us that in the Sacrament forgiveness of sins, life, and salvation are given us through these words. For where there is forgiveness of sins, there is also life and salvation.

How can bodily eating and drinking do such great things?

Certainly not just eating and drinking do these things, but the words written here: "Given and shed for you for the forgiveness of sins." These words, along with the bodily eating and drinking, are the main thing in the Sacrament. Whoever believes these words has exactly what they say: "forgiveness of sins."

Who receives this sacrament worthily?

Fasting and bodily preparation are certainly fine outward training. But that person is truly worthy and well prepared who has faith in these words: "Given and shed for you for the forgiveness of sins." But anyone who does not believe these words or doubts them is unworthy and unprepared, for the words "for you" require all hearts to believe.